SIMPLE MARIONETTES

and other wooden toys

PHILIP AND MARINDA CLAASEN

δelος

Contents

Introduction 3
Whistling woer-woers 4
Handclappers 6
Japanese broomstick puppet 8
Sparky the marionette 10
Rope climbers 12
Toys on wheels 16
Sea-animal mobiles 21
Pinkey the elephant 25
Pinocchio 28

Delos
40 Heerengracht
Cape Town
© 1989 Delos Publishers

All rights reserved. No part of this book may be reproduced or transmitted in any form or by any means, electronic or mechanical, including photocopying, recording or by any information storage and retrieval system, without the written permission of the publisher.

Photography by John Wassenaar
Sketches by Reiner Leist
Set in 10 on 11 pt Optima
Printed and bound by National Book Printers, Goodwood, Cape.
First edition 1989

ISBN 1-86826-029-1

Introduction

This book offers a collection of toys for children of all ages. These toys will dance in the wind, scramble up ropes, make a noise or follow faithfully along behind children and their bicycles. There are brightly coloured dragons, monkeys, circus elephants, snails and clowns and they will give as much joy to the maker as to the receiver.

In this age of plastic and mass production, handmade goods are becoming increasingly popular. A child takes pleasure in knowing that his toy is unique and that nowhere in the world is there another one exactly like his. If he has also helped to make the toy, he will have much more respect for it.

Many of the toys can be made from off-cuts of wood and the most expensive items will be some paint and a few brushes. Most of the materials required are inexpensive and easily available in hardware stores. There is no need for dad to be an expert woodworker or have access to a vast, well-equipped workshop. Basic tools such as a drill, fretsaw, hammer, screwdriver and a pair of pliers will be adequate.

This book contains twelve different projects which can be tackled by the whole family. Once dad and junior have done the sawing and sanding, everyone else can help with the painting.

However, these are not instant toys that can be made in a jiffy – they will take some time. If the job is done properly, these toys will become family heirlooms and in years to come there is no reason why they shouldn't look as good as the day they were made.

Doing the painting
It will be worth your while preparing the painting surfaces properly before you start to paint. Sand the wood well and use a sanding to prevent the wood from absorbing the paint. This will make the painting so much easier. Sanding can be obtained from any hardware store. Remember to sand the wood again with fine sandpaper once the sealer has dried.

Almost any paint that is nontoxic can be used. Poster paint (obtainable from art and stationary shops) is probably the easiest. Remember that red, yellow and blue can be mixed to obtain the other colours so it isn't necessary to buy a full range. You will also need black and white paint and a few paint brushes of different sizes. (Expensive brushes are not essential – you will be able to show off a superb toy with an ordinary brush.)

Initially it is better to stick to basic bright colours like red, yellow, green and blue. These colours always look good together and they don't clash. White paint is wonderful for brightening things up and for mixing with the other colours to produce pastel shades. Use black sparingly – it is handy for faces and for outlining.

The first rule when it comes to painting toys is to forget about being realistic. Elephants can be pink, dolphins red and snails blue. There is no rule which says that toys should be painted the same on both sides. We prefer to paint the two sides differently. This is a bit like getting two toys for the price of one. It can also be tedious trying to copy the paintwork from the side that was painted first.

The photographs in the book are merely a guideline. Allow your imagination free reign. Remember that there are no rules. What is important though, is that the faces should be friendly and appealing. It is no good having a beautifully painted toy with a face that scares the children! The faces we have used are included on the drawings so you can easily trace them onto the toys. It may be a good idea to use these faces at first. Later you can design and paint your own.

Experiment with your paint and enjoy the painting. Don't skimp on the paintwork as this makes your toy unique and different. A little extra trouble taken in the painting is always rewarded. Allow the children to help; they will enjoy it and it will make them doubly proud of their unique toy.

As has been mentioned, these are not instant toys. Allow enough time for the paint to dry before applying the next coat. A little trick that helps tremendously is to paint the entire surface in one or two basic colours. For example, the shoes and pants of the clown rope climber can be painted red, his shirt yellow and the rest white. When this coat has dried, it is so much easier to paint the detail on top. Give your toy a perfect finish with a coat of glossy nontoxic varnish. If you are using glossy paint, this won't be necessary. Try not to spill paint on the back of the toy – you will have to sand it off and that can be the most boring job on earth!

You don't have to be a second Da Vinci or Michelangelo. Remember that pencils have erasers because everybody makes mistakes and there is nothing that cannot be repainted. When it comes to painting toys, there is no such thing as a fatal mistake!

Whistling woer-woers

A woer-woer is a traditional South African toy and should not need any introduction. Many of the older generation probably remember making woer-woers with buttons in their youth. This is truly a toy for the whole family — for adults a woer-woer serves much the same function as worry beads. The woer-woer *must* work — if at first it doesn't, it is unlikely that the fault lies with the toy! Keep trying!

Material needed
1 A small piece of plywood, 4 mm thick
2 Two pieces of dowelling, 10 mm thick × 50 mm long (The thickness is not really important as the dowelling is used for the handles.)
3 A piece of thin nylon string, 1 mm thick × 800 mm long
4 Paint

Instructions
1 Trace the pattern onto the plywood and cut out the woer-woer.
2 Mark the woer-woer as indicated on the drawing and drill two 2 mm holes through it.
3 Cut two 50 mm lengths of dowelling and drill two 2 mm holes through both pieces as indicated on the drawing.
4 Thread 800 mm of nylon string through the woer-woer, wind it up and test it. If it works, undo the string and paint the woer-woer in bright colours on both sides. Remember to allow the paint to dry before painting the other side.
5 Thread the string through the woer-woer once more, wind it up and pull both the dowelling handles.

Have fun!

WHISTLING WOER-WOERS

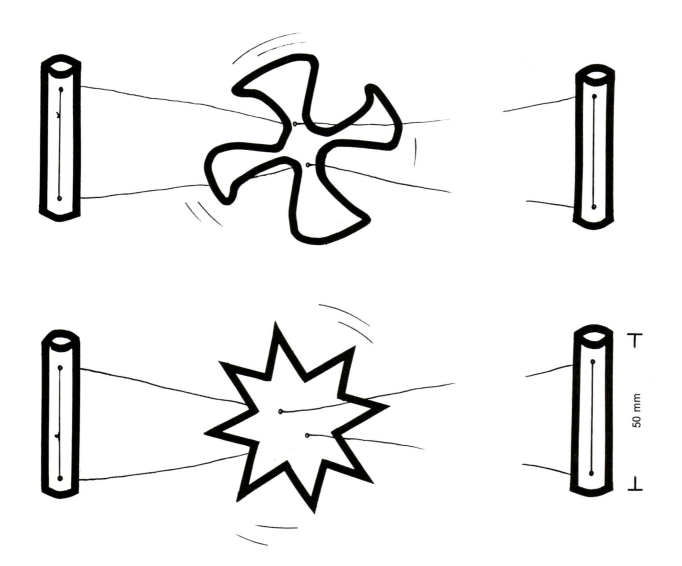

50 mm

Handclappers

Like the woer-woer this simple toy can easily be made with the minimum of effort. Toddlers especially will have endless hours of fun with this noisemaker. Mum can also use it to order coffee on a Sunday morning! The noise factor of the clapper is quite high so send the children to play outside or encourage them to use it as a simple musical instrument.

Hint: The volume of noise produced by the clapper is a function of the length of the string — a tighter knot will reduce the noise considerably!

Material needed
1 A piece of plywood, 6 mm thick
2 A colourful piece of string, 1 mm thick
3 Bright paint

Instructions
1 Trace the pattern of the two hands and handle onto the plywood.
2 Cut out the three pieces.
3 Drill 2 mm holes in both hands and the handle as indicated on the drawing.
4 Sand the plywood with fine sandpaper before painting it.
5 Paint the hands on both sides in bright colours. When the paint is dry, put one hand above the handle and the other hand below the handle. Now thread the string through the holes in the hands and the handle and make a knot. The knot should not be too tight; it must have a little play. Remember: the more play, the noisier the sound of the clapper.

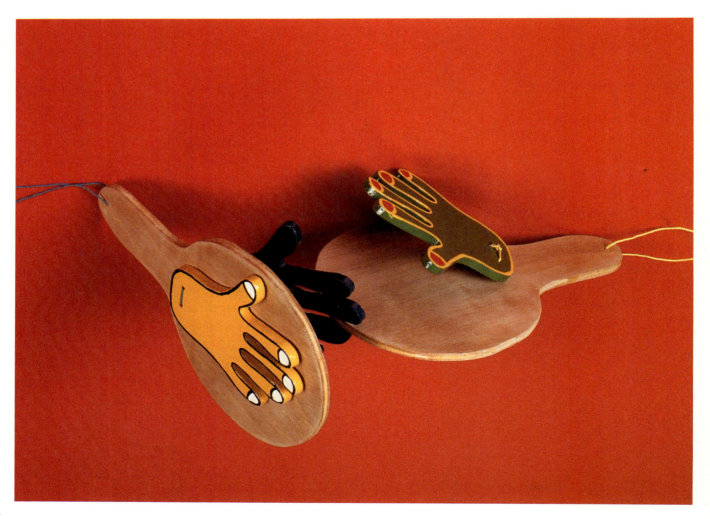

HANDCLAPPERS

Japanese broomstick puppet

This unique broomstick puppet is manipulated by a single piece of string and is capable of executing the most amazing dancing steps. Apart from its obvious love of dancing, it can sit and walk or go on all fours like a monkey. It is especially suitable for preschoolers. Like the first two projects, it can be made in a short time.

Material needed
1. A broomstick, 25 mm thick
2. A length of dowelling, 10 mm thick
3. A small piece of plywood or wood for the feet
4. Seven shoe tacks
5. Six screw-in curtain hooks
6. A length of coloured string, 1 mm thick
7. A curtain ring
8. A piece of bright material for the hat
9. Bright paint and a black pen for drawing the face

Instructions
1. Cut a 60 mm length off the broomstick.
2. Drill four 2 mm holes on either end of the broomstick for the arms and the legs – 20 mm from the top for the arms and 7 mm from the bottom for the legs.
3. Cut four 45 mm lengths of dowelling and drill holes of 1 mm × 5 mm deep in the top and the bottom of the four pieces of the cut dowel – eight holes in all.
4. Cut the feet from the plywood (15 mm × 25 mm) and drill a hole of 2 mm in each foot (see drawing).
5. Once all the components have been cut out, paint the puppet in different colours. Allow the paint to dry before assembling the puppet.
6. Screw a curtain hook into the top and bottom of each arm as well as the top of each leg.
7. Attach both feet with a shoe tack to the bottom of the legs. (Hint: put a little glue on the shoe tack to ensure that the feet do not pull out.)
8. Take a pair of pliers and close up the loop of the curtain hooks at the shoulders. Nail the arms through the loop with tacks onto the broomstick (body) – not too tightly as the arms must be able to move freely.
9. Nail the two legs and the top of the puppet's head onto the body in the same way. Fasten the one end of the string (750 mm long) to a curtain ring and fasten the other end to the nail in the head.
10. Cut out a round hat for the puppet. Remember to thread the string through the hat before glueing it onto the head.

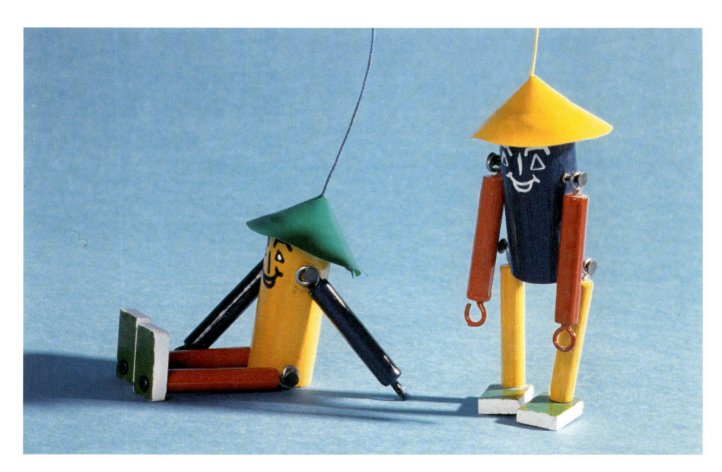

JAPANESE BROOMSTICK PUPPET

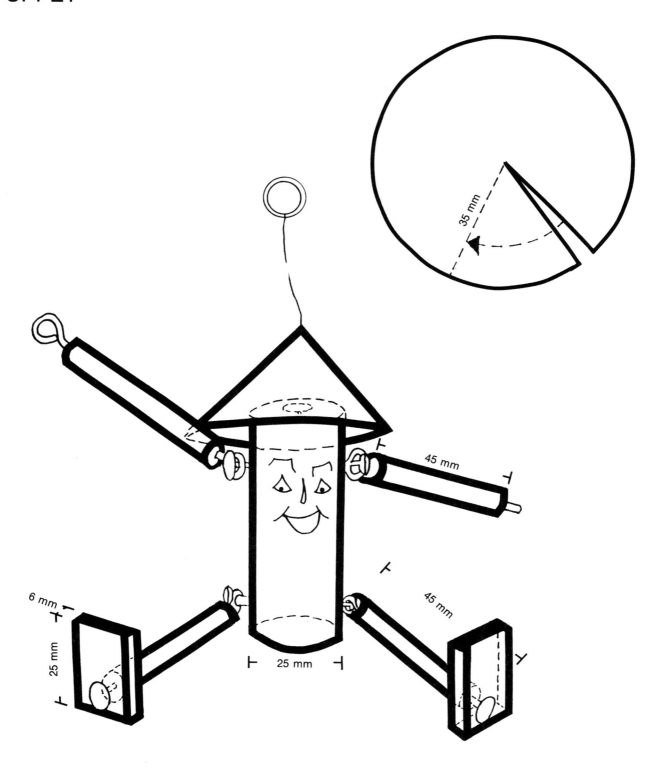

Sparky the marionette

Sparky is an eager and willing robot puppet who can't wait for his toddler friends to play with him. Unlike the broomstick puppet, his head moves independently of his body and he can walk, dance, lie down and sit. He is a little bigger than the broomstick puppet and is controlled with one string only. Sparky can be made in next to no time.

Material needed
1. A piece of timber, 15 mm thick, for the head and body
2. A piece of timber, 10 mm thick, for the feet
3. 1 m braided cord, 2 mm thick
4. 45 coloured plastic beads (available from most hobby or bead shops)
5. A length of string, 1 mm thick
6. A curtain ring
7. Four shoe tacks

Instructions
1. Trace the pattern onto the wood and cut out the head and body – the head 60 mm × 30 mm and the body 60 mm × 70 mm.
2. Drill holes of 3 mm as indicated on the drawing
   a. through the middle of the top of the head (for the neck),
   b. in the middle on top of the body, 15 mm deep (for the bottom of the neck),
   c. aan albei sykante van die lyf (10 mm van bo × 15
   c. on either side of the body, 10 mm from the top × 15 mm deep (for the arms) and
   d. at the bottom of the body, 15 mm deep (for the legs).
3. From the 10 mm timber, cut out the feet (30 mm × 60 mm) and drill a hole of 3 mm in each. Note: all the holes to be drilled are clearly indicated on the drawing.
4. Paint the puppet and allow the parts to dry before assembling it.
5. Cut 100 mm of the braided cord and tie a knot at one end. Thread the cord through the hole in the top of the head and then through three beads to form the neck. Nail the neck with a shoe tack to the top of the body. (The head, neck and body are now assembled.)
6. Cut 150 mm of the cord, tie a knot at one end and thread it through the hole drilled in the foot (the knot should be under the foot). Thread the cord through fifteen beads and nail the other end to the bottom of the body with a shoe tack. Do the same for the other leg.
7. Cut 90 mm of the cord, tie a knot at one end and thread it through six beads. Nail the other end with a shoe tack to the body to form the arm. Do the same for the other arm.
8. Take a 500 mm length of the thin string, tie one end to the curtain ring and other end to the knot on top of the head.

aan die gordynring vas. Knoop die ander kant van die tou om die knoop van die nylontou bo-op die kop.

Rope climbers

Rope climbers are traditional toys that appear in different shapes and sizes all over the world. Apparently sailors on long sea voyages used to while away the time carving these ingenious little toys. Cedric the Clown and Moya the Monkey will scurry up the ropes threaded through their hands if you pull them rhythmically. The longer the rope, the higher they will climb.

Material needed
1. A piece of plywood, 6 mm thick
2. A piece of dowelling, 10 mm thick and 150 mm long
3. 4 m braided cord, 2 mm thick
4. Eight coloured beads
5. Bright paint

Instructions
1. Trace one of the designs onto the plywood and cut it out.
2. Drill a hole of 2,5 mm at an angle of 45° through both hands (see drawing). These two holes should be drilled accurately as the braided cord must grip the holes firmly to enable the rope climber to climb the rope.
3. Sand the rope climber with fine sandpaper.
4. Drill three 3 mm holes in the dowelling as indicated on the drawing.
5. Paint the rope climber and allow it to dry before assembling it.
6. Thread 1,5 m braided cord through each hand. Note: braided cord gives the best results. Thread the cord for the hands through the two outer holes of the dowelling.
7. Take a short piece of cord and thread it through the middle hole in the dowelling. This should form a loop from which the rope climber must hang. The dowelling must move freely. Although the beads are optional, they give the toy a professional finish.
8. Hang the rope climber against a wall. Pull the one string and then the other and he will start climbing. (It is bit like milking a cow.) The sky's the limit!

Toys on wheels

Toddlers derive enormous pleasure from dragging things behind them. These pull-along toys on wheels are perfect and will work equally well behind a tricycle! There are three designs: Solly the Snail, William the Dragon and Peter the Pony. Since they are all made in much the same way, they are discussed together.

Materials needed
1. A piece of wood, 19 mm thick
2. A length of dowelling, 6 mm thick
3. Four 50 mm plastic, nylon or wooden wheels with a 6 mm shaft. (Wooden wheels can be cut from 12 mm wood. We prefer to use nylon wheels, available commercially as trolley wheels.)
4. Coloured string
5. A screw-in curtain hook
6. Two coloured pipe cleaners for the snail
7. A piece of plastic or fabric for the dragon's tongue
8. Four drawing pins

Instructions
1. Trace the pattern onto the wood and cut it out.
2. Drill two 6 mm holes through the wood (see drawings). These holes must be the same size as the shaft of the wheels you are using. Note: the snail requires two extra 2 mm holes (5 mm deep) in his head for the antennae.
3. Sand the toy and paint it. Remember that there are no rules which say it should look the same on both sides.
4. Cut two pieces of dowelling, approximately 80 mm in length. The two dowels are the axles for the wheels; the length depends on the type of wheels being used.
5. Push both pieces of dowelling through the holes in the body: Note: the axles must fit tightly – the wheels must turn, not the axles. If there is any play, glue the axles to the toy.
6. Put the wheels on and ensure that they turn freely. To prevent them from falling off, you can press drawing pins with a little glue on them into each end of the axles. Coloured plastic-topped drawing pins look most attractive.
7. For the snail you can make two antennae with the pipe cleaners and glue them into the holes drilled in the head. The dragon's tongue can be cut from material and glued into the mouth.
8. Screw the curtain hook into the toy's head, fasten 1 m of thin coloured string to the curtain hook and, hey presto, another toy completed!

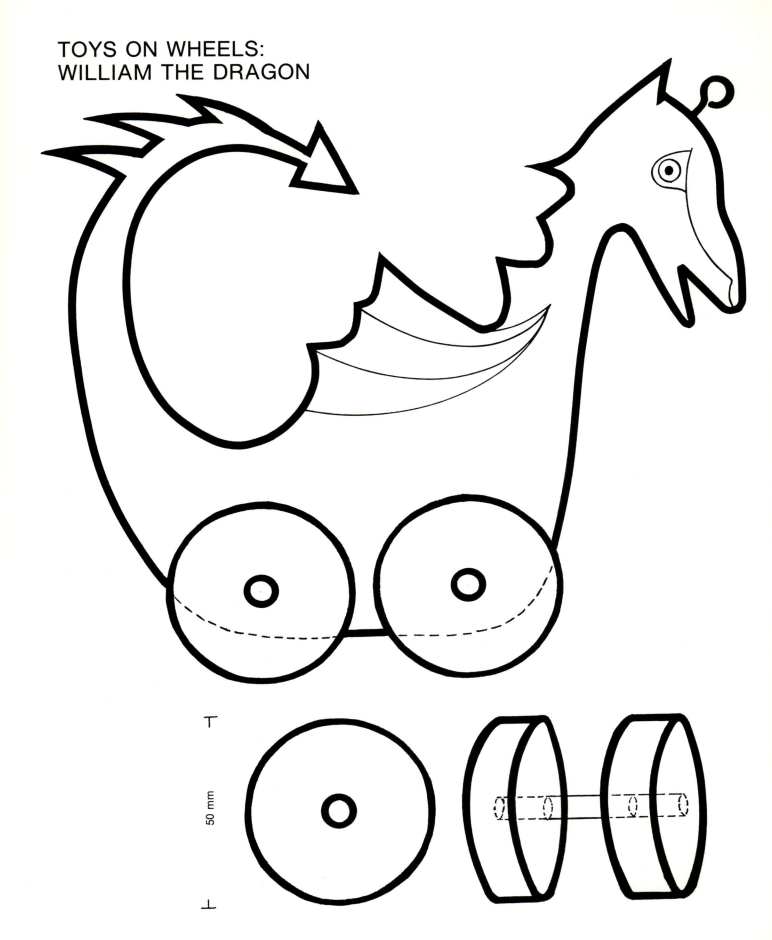

TOYS ON WHEELS:
WILLIAM THE DRAGON

50 mm

PETER THE PONY

SOLLY THE SNAIL

Sea-animal mobile

The sea-animal mobile is a beautiful decoration for hanging above a baby's cot and holding the infant's interest. Older children can learn the names of the animals while looking after the baby. The six different animals are a dolphin, a whale, a goldfish, a penguin, a guppy and a sea horse.

Material needed
1. A piece of plywood, 6 mm thick
2. A length of dowelling, 10 mm thick
3. A nut and bolt, 3 mm thick × 40 mm long
4. Thin coloured string
5. A thin nail or curtain hook for hanging the mobile from the ceiling
6. Bright paint
7. Brightly coloured wooden beads (optional)

Instructions
1. Trace the six designs of the animals onto the plywood and cut them out.
2. Drill a 2 mm hole in each of the animals as indicated on the drawing.
3. Paint the animals on both sides in bright colours and leave them to dry.
4. Cut three 300 mm lengths of dowelling and in the middle of each drill a hole of 3 mm.
5. Drill a hole of 2 mm (5 mm from the ends) in each of the dowels.
6. Push the bolt through the hole drilled in the middle of the dowels and tighten the nut at the bottom.
7. Tie a 750 mm length of string to each of the animals and thread the pieces of string through the holes at the end of the dowels. Pull the pieces of string together and thread them through a wooden bead or knot them together. Make sure that all the dowels are horizontal. An interesting effect can be achieved if all the strings are not precisely the same length and the animals do not hang at the same height. Suggestion: decorate the mobile brightly with coloured wooden beads. Although the beads are not functional, they give a professional finish.

GOLDFISH

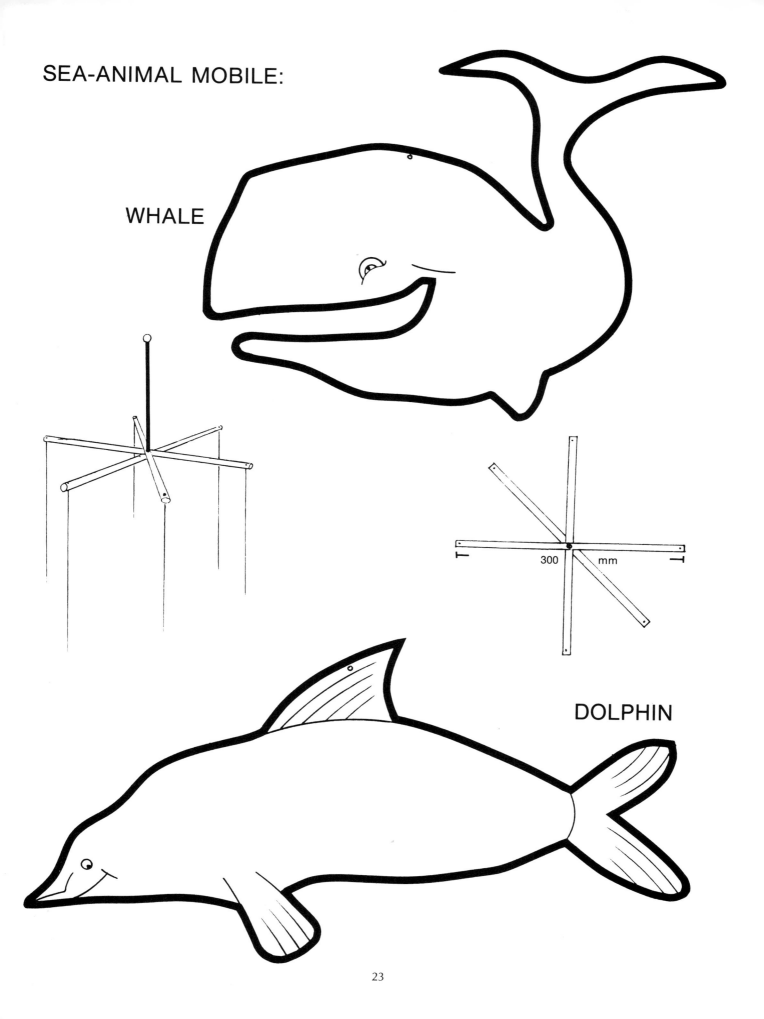

Pinkey the elephant

This cute little elephant is the most complicated puppet in the book and is most suitable for children between the ages of seven and ten. Although it is quite simple to make Pinkey, it will take quite a while to master his movements. The idea is to teach Pinkey to walk and dance to the beat of the music.

Material needed
1. A piece of timber, 19 mm thick, for the body
2. A piece of timber, 25 mm thick, for the feet
3. A length of 8 mm thick string
4. One screw-in curtain hook
5. A length of dowelling, 10 mm thick, for the control stick
6. Thin string or fishing line, 1 mm thick
7. A nut and bolt, 3 mm thick × 25 mm long
8. Two shoe tacks
9. Cold glue

Instructions

Body and Feet
1. Trace the drawing of the elephant's body onto the timber and cut it out.
2. Drill a hole of 8 mm through the lower part of the body. Screw the curtain hook into the top of the body (see drawing).
3. Cut out four circles with a diameter of 50 mm from the 25 mm timber for the feet. Glue two circles on top of each other to form one foot. Drill a hole of 8 mm (10 mm deep) in the middle on top of each foot.
4. Paint the body and feet and leave to dry. Cut a 200 mm length of the 8 mm string and thread it through the hole in the elephant's body. Dip both ends of the string in glue and nail each end of the string into the feet with a shoe tack.

Control stick
1. Cut a length of 200 mm (dowel A) and one of 100 mm (dowel B) off the dowelling. Place dowel A and dowel B over one another.
2. Drill a 3 mm hole through both dowels in the centre where they cross and bolt them together as indicated in the drawing.
3. Drill a 2 mm hole about 5 mm from the front end of dowel A.
4. Drill a 2 mm hole in the left and right side of dowel B (5 mm from each end).

Assembling the Puppet
1. Take two pieces of thin string, 1 m in length, and fasten them to each of the elephant's ankles — make the knots properly to ensure that they will not come undone.
2. Tie another metre of thin string to the curtain ring on the elephant's head. There are now three loose ends of string.
3. Tie the string from the elephant's body to the hole drilled in dowel A, the string from the left foot to the hole in the left side of the control stick and the string from the right foot to the hole in the right side of the control stick. Remember: the strings to the feet must be the same length — if one of the strings is not tight enough, adjust the string on the control stick or Pinkey will not be able to perform all the tricks.

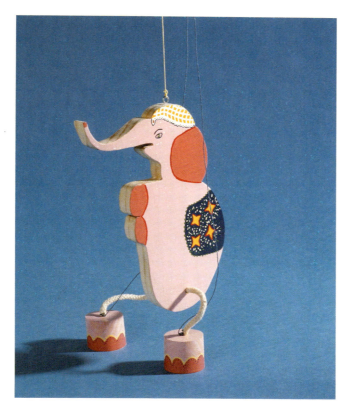

PINKEY THE ELEPHANT

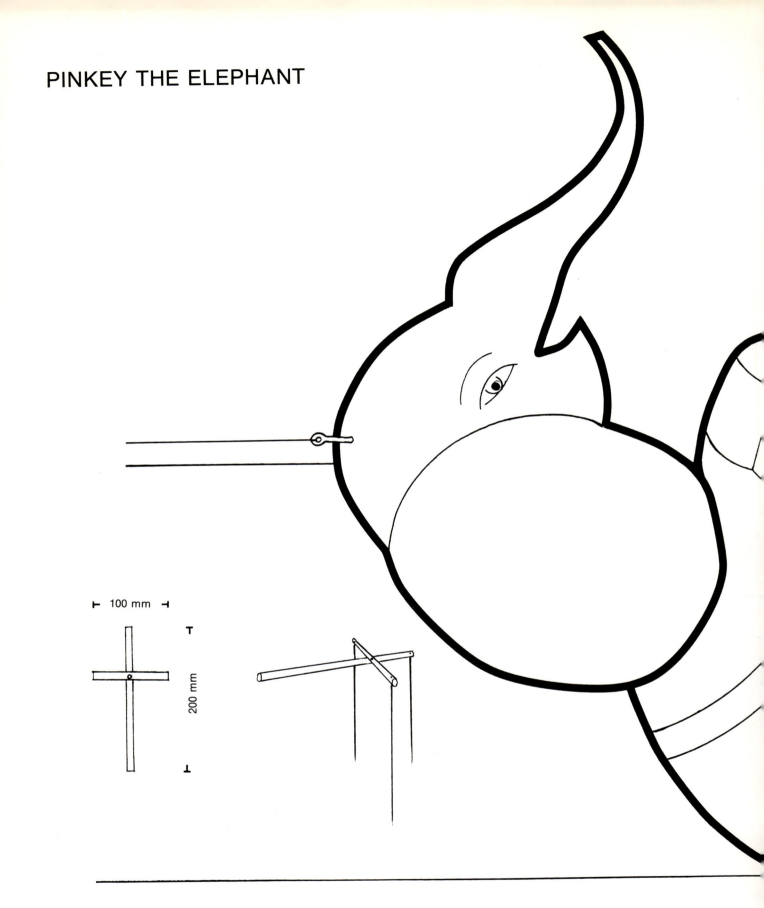

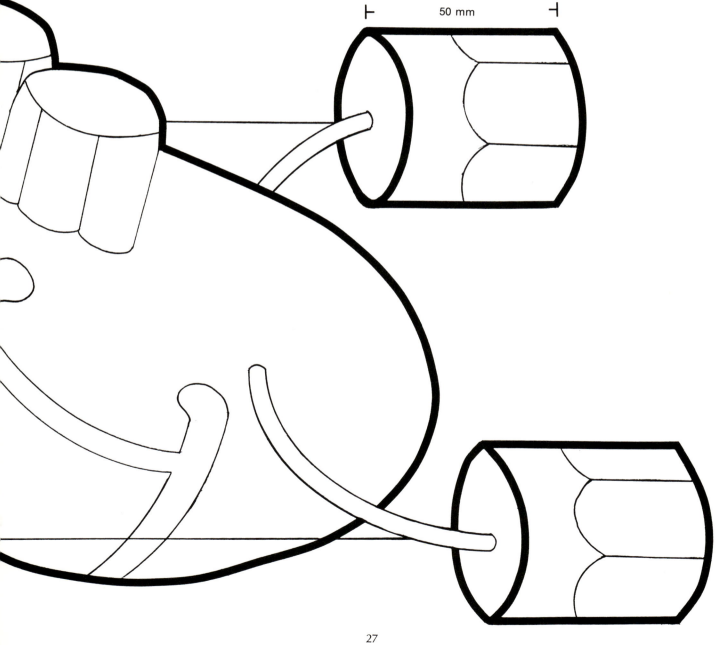

Pinocchio

This world famous little fellow from Italy with his prominent nose needs no introduction. Whereas other puppets are manipulted by strings, Pinocchio simply has a control stick fitted in the back of his head. It will take a little longer to make this toy, but the end result should be worthwhile.

Material needed

1. A solid piece of timber, 50 mm thick, for the head (A finial for the end of a curtain rod — available from most hardware stores — can also be used.)
2. A piece of scrap timber, 20 mm thick, for the body
3. A piece of scrap timber, 10 mm thick, for the hands and feet
4. Two lengths of dowelling 10 mm thick, for the nose, neck, arms and legs and control stick
5. Ten short nails, 1 mm thick
6. An off-cut of leather or any thick fabric for the elbows and knees
7. Suitable wool for the hair, preferably in shades of brown and beige to match Pinocchio's outfit.
8. A piece of dark blue, green, red and white felt for Pinocchio's clothing, as well as two buttons for his shirt
9. Cold glue
10. Red and white paint for the mouth
11. Two eyes, 10 mm in diameter (The eyes can be bought at a hobby shop, but can be painted with black and white paint if unavailable.)
12. Colourful ribbon for the neck
13. Thin binding wire, 1 mm thick
14. A short piece of string, 2 mm thick

Instructions

Head, Nose and Neck

1. Turn a head on a lathe. (It should be 180 mm in circumference.) Otherwise, cut off the top and bottom of a finial so that it forms a ball.
2. Mark the middle of Pinocchio's head for the nose.
3. Drill a hole of 10 mm through the head.
4. Drill a hole 10 mm × 10 mm at the bottom of the head for the neck.
5. Cut two 30 mm lengths of dowelling and dip one end of each in glue.
6. Carefully hammer the one dowel 15 mm into the hole that has been drilled for Pinocchio's nose — the part that sticks out for the nose must be 15 mm long.
7. Hammer the glued end of the second dowel 5 mm into the neck.

Body

1. Trace the body on the drawing onto the timber and cut out the body.
2. Drill a hole 10 mm × 5 mm in the top of the body.
3. Don't glue the neck to the body yet. Drill a hole 3 mm × 20 mm in the left and right sides of Pinocchio's body.
4. Use the same bit to drill two holes 3 mm × 20 mm in the lower part of Pinocchio's body (see drawing).

Hands and feet

1. Trace the hands and the feet onto the timber and cut them out.
2. Drill a hole 1 mm × 10 mm in each of Pinocchio's wrists. The holes in the feet are done the same way, but they must be drilled right through.

Upper legs

1. Cut two 30 mm lengths off the dowelling for the upper legs.
2. Saw a 5 mm groove along the centre of the lower surface of each side of the upper legs.
3. Drill a hole 3 mm × 5 mm on the top side of each upper leg.
4. Take two 40 mm lengths of string, dip one end of each in glue and push them into the holes which have just been drilled in the legs.
5. Wait for the glue to dry and nail each upper leg into the holes in the body with a 2 mm nail. The upper legs are now attached to Pinocchio's body.

Lower legs

1. Cut two 50 mm lengths of dowelling.
2. Drill a hole of 1 mm × 10 mm in the lower part of each.
3. Saw a 5 mm groove along the centre of the top surface of each lower leg.
4. Glue the lower legs (i.e. the drilled side) to the feet.
5. Push 20 mm of binding wire through the feet into the lower legs. The wire reinforces the glue joint between the lower legs and the feet.
6. Cut two pieces of leather 10 mm × 20 mm. Glue along one side of each piece and fit it into the groove of the lower legs. Note: don't glue the lower legs to the upper legs yet or you will not be able to put the pants on.

Upper arms

1. Cut two 30 mm lengths of dowelling.
2. Drill a hole of 3 mm × 10 mm in the top of each arm.
3. Saw a 5 mm groove along the lower surface of each arm.
4. Take two 40 mm lengths of string, dip one end of each into glue and push them into the holes which have just been drilled. Wait for the glue to dry and nail each upper arm into the holes in the body.

Lower arms

1. Cut two 30 mm lengths of dowelling.
2. Drill a hole 1 mm × 10 mm in the lower part of each lower arm.
3. Saw a 5 mm groove in the top part of each lower arm.
4. Push two mm lengths of binding wire into the holes in the lower arms and attach them with glue to the holes in the hands.
5. Wait for the glue to dry. Cut two pieces of leather 10 mm × 20 mm. Glue along one side of each piece and fit it into the grooves. Note: do not glue the lower arms to the upper arms yet or you will not be able to put the jacket on.

Face

1. Glue Pinocchio's eyes on and paint his mouth with red and white paint.
2. Glue the wool onto his head. Wait for it to dry and then glue the hat on.
3. Use enough glue to secure the hair and hat firmly. Apply glue to the neck and attach the head to the body.

Clothing

Make the clothing out of felt — it is really quite simple.

1. Glue a piece of white felt onto Pinocchio's chest and glue two or three buttons onto it when it is dry.
2. See if mum can make the jacket, trousers and hat on the sewing machine – a bit of embroidery on the jacket is quite effective.
3. Dress Pinocchio in his trousers and jacket and glue the lower and upper legs to one another.
4. Do the same for the lower and upper arms. To prevent wet glue from spoiling his clothes, use a clothespeg to keep the fabric out of the way.

Last but not least
Once the paint and glue are dry, cut Pinocchio's hair and tie a bow round his neck. Cut a 150 mm length of dowelling and push it into the hole at the back of his head. Use this dowel as a control to make him sit jump and dance. Children will find Pinocchio a wonderful companion.

PINOCCHIO

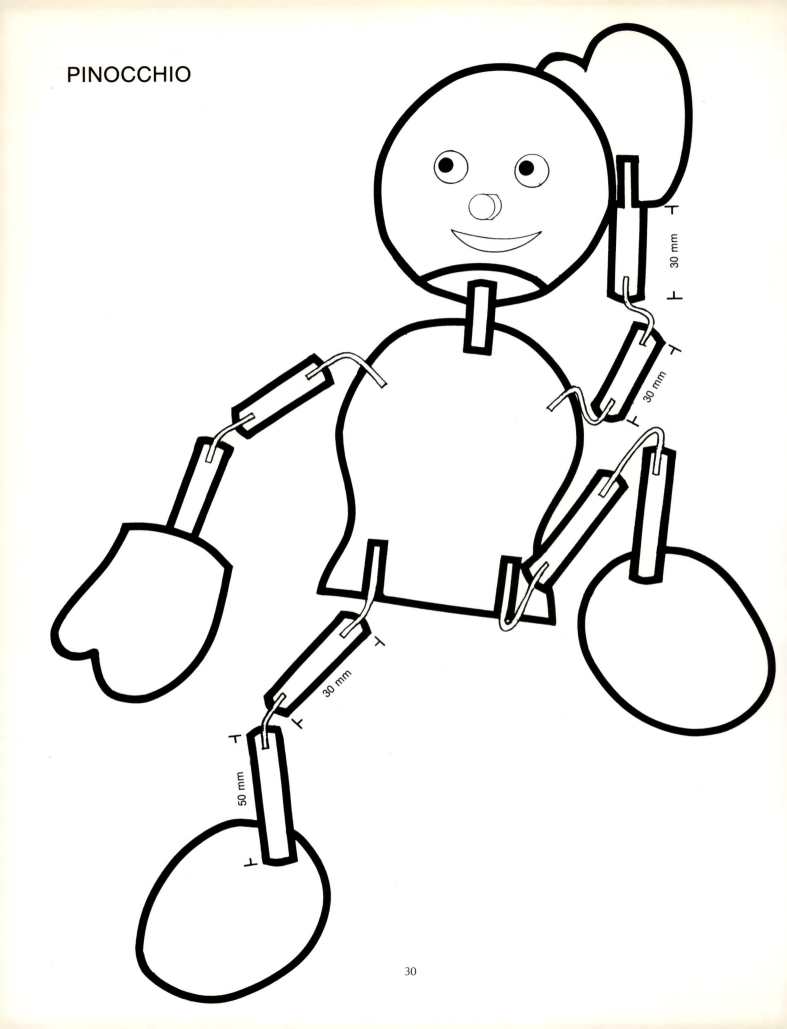

PINOCCHIO'S CLOTHES

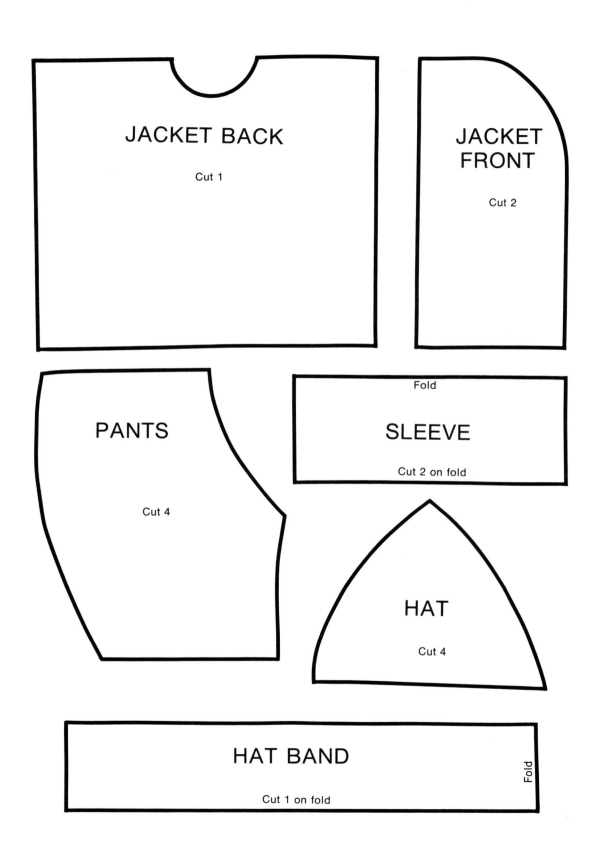